2 words 2 live by

mark madden

**You can change your life—
two words at a time**

House of Madness Publishing

2 WORDS 2 LIVE BY

House of Madness Publishing

Copyright © 2015 by Mark Madden

All Rights Reserved

Copy Editor: Kim Catanzarite
Cover Design: David Locke
Interior Design: David Locke and Mark Madden

All rights reserved worldwide. No part of this book may be reproduced in any form by any means without the express permission of the author. This includes reprints, excerpts, photocopying, recording, or any future means of reproducing text.

For Biblical references:
THE HOLY BIBLE, NEW INTERNATIONAL VERSION®, NIV® Copyright © 1973, 1978, 1984, 2011 by Biblica, Inc.® Used by permission.
All rights reserved worldwide.

For information about special discounts for bulk purchases or to book Mark Madden for a speaking engagement, please contact House of Madness Publishing at 855-505-5799 or info@twowordsbook.com.

PRINTED IN THE UNITED STATES OF AMERICA

ISBN 978-0-9899884-0-7

June 2015

First Edition

www.twowordsbook.com

Names: Madden, Mark, 1961-
Title: 2 words 2 live by / Mark Madden.
Other Titles: Two words to live by
Description: [Anderson, South Carolina] : House of Madness Publishing, [2015]
Identifiers: ISBN 978-0-9899884-0-7
Subjects: LCSH: Conduct of life--Miscellanea. | Maxims. | Affirmations. | Motivation (Psychology)
Classification: LCC BF637.C5 M34 2015 | DDC 158.1--dc23

DEDICATION

This book is dedicated to all veterans—past, present, and future. May you always be honored, respected, admired, and remembered.

This book is also dedicated to the memory of the individuals listed below. These amazing people have taught me some of life's most important lessons: unfailing courage in the face of overwhelming obstacles, infinite persistence and determination, a genuine passion for life, curiosity, patience, gentleness, kindness, and unconditional love. You will find their influence throughout the pages of this book.

Samuel Landon Madden
    November 20, 1933 – August 8, 1982

Patti Reneé Crump
    August 30, 1961 – November 7, 1979

Lt. Stephen R. King
    November 29, 1955 – August 13, 1983

Ivey Lynne Aycock
    September 13, 1966 – February 20, 1985

Ronnie Dale Aycock
    January 22, 1961 – April 26, 2002

Kilian James Jones
    January 11, 1964 – February 22, 1998

Jill Dunlap
    September 24, 1967 – January 29, 1986

Michael Odum
    March 26, 1953 – January 10, 2003

Tanner Odum
    April 15, 1978 – September 1, 2008

Wendie Cheek
    April 17, 1978 – October 5, 2013

Jacob Jameson
    February 8, 1988 – February 23, 2011

Mike Cole
    February 27, 1961 – May 24, 1998

Catherine Renee Montgomery
    January 12, 1961 – April 10, 2015

INTRODUCTION

If you are like me, you've probably read many so-called "self-help" books. And like me you have probably come to the end of one of those three- or four-hundred page tomes unsure of how to apply the concepts and theories espoused in those books to your daily life.

In writing 2 Words 2 Live By, I took a straightforward, simple approach to self-improvement. It's easy for me to commit two words to the forefront of my thoughts for a day, a week, or even longer and to use those two words to establish a new thought pattern, to create a new habit or in certain instances to remove something negative from my behavior. I think it'll be easy for you as well.

The fifty two-word phrases in this book run the gamut of topics—from the practical items (Change Oil) to the physical (Eat Right) to those that delve deeper (Don't Judge).

As you look in the table of contents, you'll find the two-word phrases organized into five disciplines of life: physical, mental, practical, social, and spiritual. Each life discipline is uniquely color-coded throughout the book. Additionally, the life discipline is listed near the page number on the left-hand pages of the book for easy reference. Take a moment review the organization of the book. You can then decide how you want to tackle the book: sequentially, by life discipline, or perhaps just randomly.

My suggestion is to take a single two-word phrase and place it foremost in your mind for a week. After a year, you will have gone through all fifty two-word phrases.

My sincere hope is that you will be able to use this book to change your life—two words at a time.

Good Luck.

Have Fun.

CONTENTS

PHYSICAL	MENTAL
10 Laugh Often	**12** Dream Big
14 Stay Healthy	**34** Keep Learning
26 Breathe Deeply	**54** Play Music
36 Sleep Well	**58** Get Help
46 Eat Right	**64** Stay Calm
62 Don't Smoke	**68** Control Stress
72 Walk Daily	**88** Don't Worry
80 Sun Block	**94** Expect Nothing
90 Drink Water	**96** Be Positive
102 Get Checkups	**106** Persevere Always

PRACTICAL	**SOCIAL**	**SPIRITUAL**
16 Live Modestly	**18** Have Manners	**20** Love Others
22 Buckle Up	**28** Encourage Someone	**24** Count Blessings
30 Pursue Adventure	**38** Give Credit	**32** Don't Judge
40 Set Goals	**44** Never Complain	**42** Be Kind
50 Road Trip	**52** Be Tolerant	**48** Forgive Unconditionally
66 Change Oil	**56** Appreciate Others	**76** Be Patient
74 Look Ahead	**60** Smile Often	**82** Don't Envy
78 Save Regularly	**70** Give Everything	**92** Make Peace
86 Get Outside	**84** Build Up	**104** Gain Wisdom
98 Recycle Everything	**100** Give Back	
108 Baby Steps		

"Always laugh when you can, it is cheap medicine."

— George Gordon Byron

PHYSICAL

LAUGH OFTEN

10

Laugh a ha ha ha

TAKE ACTION

Share a (funny) joke with a friend.

It is true. Laughter is the best medicine. Laughter can have profound effects on our physical and emotional health.

Laughter is beneficial to your physical health. It relaxes the entire body. Studies reveal that laughter can trigger the release of endorphins, the hormones that make you feel happy. A vigorous laugh can increase your blood flow, which supports healthy heart and lung function. Research indicates that a healthy sense of humor may help protect you from a heart attack.

Laughter is also very beneficial to your emotional well-being. We genuinely feel better after a hearty laugh because it reduces stress, and who doesn't need less stress? Humor has the power to enhance your existing relationships and can be a positive influence when developing new relationships.

My father loved to laugh. He could find humor in just about anything and unlike many of us, he found it easy to laugh at himself. Even now, more than 30 years after his death, the comment I hear most often when his friends reminisce about him is, "I'll never forget that laugh."

Find a way to get laughter into your life. Listen to a funny radio program in your car, read the daily comics, or take a trip to a comedy club.

"Dare to live the life you have dreamed for yourself. Go forward and make your dreams come true."

— **Ralph Waldo Emerson**

MENTAL | **12** | **DREAM BIG**

Dream

TAKE ACTION

Write down your dream. List the action steps needed to accomplish the dream. Begin action step number one now.

Nothing stays the same. Life is change. Ideally, it is change for the better. A longer life, better health, more travel, higher earnings.

How can you change for the better? Start by dreaming. Imagine the life you want. If you have not earned a college degree, dream that you are receiving your diploma. If you live in a small apartment, you might dream of owning your own home. If you are a struggling author, you might dream of seeing your book on the bestseller lists. Only after you dream it can you begin to make it real.

Don't be modest. Dream BIG. It will keep you motivated on a daily basis. Most people start out with big dreams, but at some point in their lives, they abandon them. Their lives become a little more mundane, a little more boring, a lot less fulfilling, and a lot less fun. If you've abandoned your dreams, dig them back up. You have the rest of your life to accomplish your dreams.

Think of a dream that you once had and take some action to make it possible.

"He who enjoys good health is rich though he knows it not."

— **Italian Proverb**

PHYSICAL — STAY HEALTHY

14

STAY

TAKE ACTION

Choose one new healthy habit such as taking a walk after dinner or adding a serving of vegetables to your lunch.

What is the most valuable asset you have? Your house? Your investment portfolio? Your pension? Certainly, these things have considerable value. But what about your health?

Your health is your most important asset and must be protected at all costs. If you lose your health, you may end up losing everything.

Good health is the foundation that allows you to be happy, energized, alert, and optimistic. Health is the key to having the freedom to accomplish what you want. When you're healthy, you can take on the world and make your dreams come true.

It is true that we live in a world where illness and disease exist. You cannot avoid all of it. Sooner or later everyone gets sick. But if you are healthy, when you get sick you'll be back in action more quickly. You won't be sidelined for as long as you could be if you were not healthy.

Do something now to improve your health. Do you have habits that are detrimental to your health? Start by taking action to eliminate those habits. Once they are out of the way, you must create new habits that will maintain or enhance your health.

Every step you take toward better health is a step to a longer, happier life.

"Debt, n. An ingenious substitute for the chain and whip of the slave driver."

— **Ambrose Bierce**

PRACTICAL 16 LIVE MODESTLY

live mode$tly

TAKE ACTION

Develop a realistic plan to reduce your debt and maximize savings.

Most people want to be financially independent—maybe not super rich—but comfortable enough to avoid day-to-day monetary worries.

Why then do so many of us continually outlive our means? Why is it that when we move up on the earnings ladder, we also feel the need to move up on the spending ladder? The earning more to spend more cycle is a vicious one, and it leads not to financial freedom, but to a form of slavery. You become a slave to your income, debt, and possessions.

The solution is to live modestly. Live well below your means. Maximize your savings. We've all heard the stories of folks who lived on modest incomes only to leave small fortunes to charities, universities, and relatives. Consider the story of Roberta Langtry. Roberta was known as a frugal woman, but also one who was very generous when someone was in need. When she died, she left $3.8 million to the Nature Conservatory—money that she had saved from her modest salary as an elementary school teacher. You, too, can accumulate wealth, but you can't do it by buying luxury items.

Here's an example of how to amass wealth. If your income indicates that you can afford a $300,000 home, buy a $150,000 home and pay it off in half the time (or invest the other half of the payment). At a 6 percent mortgage rate, you would save more than $323,000 on a thirty-year loan. If you invested the difference in payment at the same 6 percent rate, you would accumulate more than $750,000 in the thirty-year period. Wouldn't you rather live in a modest home and have that cash in the bank? That's true financial independence. That's true freedom.

Be free. Live modestly.

"Respect for ourselves guides our morals; respect for others guides our manners."

— **Laurence Sterne**

HAVE MANNERS

SOCIAL

18

thank you
have

TAKE ACTION

Practice the art of courtesy with everyone you meet.

Common courtesies are not very common anymore. Where, oh where, have our manners gone? Has the fast pace of the modern world rendered them null and void? Does it take too much time or effort to say please and thank you? I recently had lunch with a colleague who was much more absorbed in the virtual world of his smartphone than in our conversation. Simply stated, that's rude.

Your behavior affects everyone with whom you interact. It is much more pleasant to open the door for another person than to let it drop in his face. Manners provide little ways to show respect and consideration. They also show what you're made of. When you greet someone, you recognize the individual's existence and validate his or her worth. When you introduce yourself, you take it a step further. Respect and consideration might seem like small things, but they go a long way in displaying an honorable character.

Manners matter. The next time you leave the house, switch your cell phone to mute and put it out of sight. Instead, say hello to the people you pass on the street or in the halls of your workplace. Look up when the waitress refills your glass and thank her. Tell the guy at the newspaper stand to have a nice weekend. Connect with your fellow men and women in a respectful way, and observe how the positivity you generate fuels your day.

manners please

"Love is patient, love is kind. It does not envy, it does not boast, it is not proud. It does not dishonor others, it is not self-seeking, it is not easily angered, it keeps no record of wrongs."

— **Holy Bible: New International Version**

TAKE ACTION

Love is not just emotions; it's also actions. Do something special for a loved one today.

No man or woman can live a full life without the love of others. Does someone love you? Do you love someone? Is love a part of your daily life?

Love is a critical element in our lives—perhaps the most critical element. We all innately feel that love is essential to our well-being. Research backs up what we think we know. The United States National Library of Medicine has presented research that suggests the quality of relationships is linked to physical health. The data indicates that relationships may have as much influence on our health as do factors such as obesity, smoking, and exercise. Additionally, research from Yale University reveals that people who feel loved suffer fewer blockages in their coronary arteries.

Everyone wants to feel loved. But what about showering love upon on others? How well do you do that? Is showing love to others a part of your daily routine? Do you make it a habit to tell your spouse or children that you love them? Perhaps it's time to take inventory and make some small changes in your behavior so that loved ones will, without a doubt, know that you love them.

When you offer words and acts of love to others, it forces you to step outside of your needs and wants and consider the feelings of others. In doing this, you also give your life meaning.

Make a special effort to spread love to those around you. You'll benefit as much as they will.

"Buckle up...it makes it harder for the aliens to suck you out of the car."

— **Unknown**

TAKE ACTION

Buckle up every single time you get in your car.

Automobiles are getting safer every year. In the United States, the fatality rate on our nation's highways peaked in 1972. During that deadly year, 54,589 people were killed in auto accidents—about two deaths per 100,000 people. Currently, the death rate is about half of that.

Many factors contribute to the increased safety of automobile travel, including air bags, crash-worthy cars, drunk-driving law enforcement, and drivers' education. But experts agree that the single most important factor in reducing auto fatalities and injuries is the lap and shoulder belt, known simply as seat belts.

Buckling up is the single most important thing that you must do to be safe in your car. Seat belts are your best source of protection in an accident. Seat belts save roughly fifteen thousand lives a year. And though we are getting better at wearing them consistently, there are still many drivers who do not buckle up. According to the United States Department of Transportation, 15 to 20 percent of all drivers still do not wear seat belts. Some drivers mistakenly believe air bags alone are sufficient. They are not. Air bags are designed to work with seat belts.

The best way to stay safe—and avoid those pesky alien abductions—is to buckle up.

"Reflect upon your present blessings—of which every man has many—not on your past misfortunes, of which all men have some."

— **Charles Dickens**

COUNT BLESSINGS

24

SPIRITUAL

Count Blessings

TAKE ACTION

Focus on your blessings, not your burdens.

Sometimes we get so wrapped up in the bad stuff that's going on in the world—or our personal lives—that we fail to see the good things that happen every day. The good things have a bad habit of falling through the cracks and, like all things that don't give us trouble, we take good for granted.

We all know from experience that negatives stay with people longer than positives do, and some doctors say that lingering upon the unpleasant can be a recipe for depression. Luckily, the antidote is simple. Acknowledge life's blessings. Write down what you love about your spouse or child. Tell your sister how glad you are that she's in your life. Give thanks before a meal, and remember that not everyone in the world is eating tonight. Count your joys instead of your woes, as the Irish proverb goes, and doing so will lead to a happier life.

The Mayo Clinic reports that if we are optimistic and focus on the good things that are a part of our lives, we will be happier and may even live longer. Several other studies have concluded that those who express gratitude tend to display more positive thoughts of the future and life as a whole.

Life can be tough. It's easy to get wrapped up in negative feelings. To make sure you don't, start a gratitude journal, and each day jot down a few things for which you are grateful. Or, even simpler, before you go to sleep at night whisper thanks for three things you appreciate in your life.

1 2 3 4 5 6 7 . . .

> "For breath is life, and if you breathe well you will live long on earth."
>
> — Sanskrit Proverb

TAKE ACTION

Perform breathing exercises daily.

Breath is life itself. When a baby is born, the very first thing we celebrate is that first breath. And when our life is over, we say that we have taken our last breath. In between, the average person will take one billion breaths.

Unfortunately, most of them are shallow breaths that support life, for sure, but could be doing a lot more good. Unless you work at a job that requires serious physical exertion, you probably aren't getting the full benefits of those breaths.

The benefits of deep breathing are enormous. The website livestrong.com notes that deep breathing reduces stress and blood pressure, and releases endorphins (the feel-good hormones) into your body. Deep breathing also helps clear your mind so you can focus. Deep breathing carries more oxygen to your cells than normal breathing. This oxygen is vital to removing waste from the body and purifying the blood.

To reap the benefits of deep breathing, practice the following exercise a few times a day.

Breathe in slowly and deeply through your nose for a count of five seconds, inhaling as much air as you can. Hold your breath for a count of three seconds (this allows the oxygen to be fully absorbed into your cells). Exhale through your mouth for a count of eight to ten seconds, expelling all of the air in your lungs. Repeat the entire process several times.

Do this exercise daily, and you'll notice a difference in no time.

"Instruction does much, but encouragement does everything."

— Johann Wolfgang von Goethe

ENCOURAGE SOMEONE

28

SOCIAL

Encourage

you rock great job

TAKE ACTION

Find a way to encourage someone this week.

Everyone has a memory from childhood when an adult, mom or dad or a teacher, offered words of encouragement. Perhaps a school problem was difficult, or you were learning to ride a bike for the first time, or a thoughtless friend hurt your feelings. The pain of despair was no doubt made easier by the encouragement you received. Because someone provided a positive word or deed, you were able to pick yourself up and try again. It was a wonderful feeling.

Adults need encouragement too. Challenges come to people of all ages, and everyone becomes discouraged now and then. The boss is too demanding. The test you must pass is difficult. Friends are not supportive. You're nervous about a presentation you must give to a room of business people.

Encouragement can have a significant effect on a person's life: a compliment on a job well done, a kind word after a romantic breakup, a helping hand when a friend is in need. Your encouragement will make a difference for the better. It could even change someone's life.

Someone wonderful

> "I love to sail forbidden seas and land on barbarous coasts."
>
> — **Herman Melville**

TAKE ACTION

Start planning your next adventure now.

In every person's life, a certain amount of drudgery is to be expected. You commute to work, clean the house, take out the trash, change the diapers, balance the checkbook. These are daily events, and most are unavoidable.

A life devoted to nothing but drudgery quickly dulls the spirit and dampens a person's sense of fun. Each new day is not an opportunity for excitement, but just another monotonous ticking away of time.

How to put an end to the monotony? Pursue adventure. There's excitement in adventures, big and small. Adventure is what makes our fondest memories. It is what you (and your children) will remember many years from now.

I enjoy adventures of all kinds. When I was in my mid-twenties, I learned to fly an airplane. I've rappelled off a 300-foot sheer cliff. I've ridden a bicycle across the state of Iowa. My current adventure is learning to surf.

Adventure can take many forms. Some obvious activities include rock climbing, whitewater rafting, and traveling to exotic lands. How about skydiving or snorkeling on a Caribbean reef? If you can afford these things, go for it. If not, pursue adventure simply by changing up your routine. Go for a hike, take your children to the local arcade, plan a treasure hunt. You can pursue adventure in many different ways. New and inexpensive adventures lay just outside your door. Go out there and get them.

"The more one judges, the less one loves."

— **Honore de Balzac**

DON'T

TAKE ACTION

Pay close attention to your conversations and your private thoughts. When you find yourself judging someone, stop.

Most people are familiar with the Biblical words, "Judge not, that ye be not judged." It's one of those universal maxims that people have tucked away in the back of their minds. It's a powerful tonic.

Unfortunately, judging others seems to be ingrained in human nature. How many times a day do you make snap judgments about the people you encounter based on what they are wearing, where they live, or what they do for a living? How many times have you made a judgment about another person's personal trials and troubles based only on what you think you know?

Here are two reasons never to judge others:

One, in most instances we do not have enough information about other people or their situations to make a fair judgment. It's easy to take sides in a conflict that involves others. Resist that temptation. Remain neutral. There are always two (or more) sides to a story, and, unfortunately, the truth is usually stuck somewhere in the middle.

Two, people are imperfect. We bring our issues, prejudices, and skeletons to bear in our judgment of others. We're all fighting our own battles, and most of us simply cannot make an unbiased assessment of another person's situation.

Don't judge. Replace judgment with compassion, empathy, and support.

"Learning is an ornament in prosperity, a refuge in adversity, and a provision in old age."

— **Aristotle**

TAKE ACTION

Explore some new learning opportunities this week.

The minute we are born we begin to learn about our environment and ourselves. We learn how to eat and walk. We learn that fire is hot and toys are fun. Our brains absorb new information every minute as we grow and connect with the world.

Some people reach a certain age, and they become complacent. They think they have everything figured out. They stop learning. But whether they realize it or not, the moment they stop learning is the moment they stop growing. In order to live a productive, happy, dynamic life, one must continue to grow.

At every age, humans have the capacity to learn something new. To challenge your mind is as important to your brain as exercise is to your body. The benefits are measurable. According to the experts at WebMD, expanding your knowledge and challenging your mind are some of the most important things you can do to stave off Alzheimer's and other age-related diseases of the mind.

There are many ways a person can continue learning. You can read books, take a course from a community or technical college, or become an apprentice to a craftsman. Learn to play a new game. Volunteer to teach someone to read (it will teach you many things, too). Find ways to make learning a lifelong process.

Learning

"There is a time for many words, and there is also a time for sleep."

— **Homer**

TAKE ACTION

Here's a novel idea. You have an alarm to wake you up. Set one to tell you when to go to sleep. Ensure there's at least seven hours in between the two.

On January 28th, 1986, the space shuttle Challenger exploded 73 seconds after launch, claiming the lives of all seven astronauts. The subsequent Presidential Commission Report stated the following in the Human Factor Analysis of the accident, "certain key managers obtained only minimal sleep the night before." While the lack of sleep was not the primary cause of the accident, it was important enough to be included in the report.

Like the managers for that ill-fated shuttle mission, few people regularly get enough sleep. Schools begin early in the morning. Long commutes to work mean adults have to get up hours before they need to be at their desks. Evening hours with the family are precious, so everyone stays up too late. What's worse, our society stigmatizes people who sleep. We hear plenty of stories about go-getters who survive on four or five hours a night. What we don't hear so much about are the stories about those who drop dead from heart attacks or strokes at an early age. According to the American Academy of Sleep Medicine, chronic sleep deprivation can potentially have serious consequences, including obesity, diabetes, and heart disease. These issues can ultimately lead to a shorter life span.

The benefits of sleep are equally compelling. Sleep allows the body and mind to refresh. Getting the proper amount of sleep reduces stress, improves your memory, and keeps your heart healthy.

Tonight, turn off the TV, snuggle up in bed, and get your well-deserved forty winks. For most people, that's between seven and nine hours. After a good night's sleep, you'll be more alert and less likely to nod off. You may even live longer.

Well

"Leadership consists of nothing but taking responsibility for everything that goes wrong and giving your subordinates credit for everything that goes well."

— **Dwight D. Eisenhower**

GIVE CREDIT

SOCIAL

TAKE ACTION

Examine your words and actions in the workplace and at home. Ensure you are giving credit when and where it's due.

You wouldn't steal your neighbor's car, would you? Or take money from the cash register at work? How about robbing a stranger on the street? Of course you wouldn't, because taking something that doesn't belong to you is a crime.

Unfortunately, at work and in everyday life, many people take credit for things they didn't do, or just as bad, they fail to give credit to the person who did them. At work, a thoughtless manager takes his assistant's idea and presents it as his own. At school, a student copies a paper off the Internet and signs her name to it. A parent celebrates his kid's victory in basketball by exclaiming, "I taught him everything he knows."

When we give credit where it is due, we are staying true to ourselves and contributing to the positive energy in our lives and the lives of those around us. When we acknowledge the contributions of others, we increase their self-confidence, raise their spirits, and earn their loyalty. True leaders concern themselves with the outcome rather than credit or fame.

In our society, personal achievement is paramount. However, no man (or woman) is an island. There is no such thing as "self-made". We all have been motivated, mentored, developed, and otherwise helped by many people who have crossed our paths. We should never underestimate (or under appreciate) the influence other people have made in our journey through this adventure called life.

"When it is obvious that the goals cannot be reached, don't adjust the goals, adjust the action steps."

— **Confucius**

SET GOALS

40

PRACTICAL

Set

TAKE ACTION

Set a new goal and take the first steps necessary to accomplish that goal.

Before a special joint session of Congress on May 25, 1961, President John F. Kennedy announced the dramatic and ambitious goal of sending an American safely to the moon before the end of the decade. On July 20, 1969, that goal was reached when Apollo 11 commander Neil Armstrong stepped off the lunar module's ladder and onto the moon's surface.

When you want to get something accomplished, set a goal. It doesn't have to be as lofty as going to the moon. The best goals are the ones that are achievable. If you want to lose weight, begin by setting a goal of five pounds. If you want to run a marathon, set a goal of running a mile. If you want to date a special person, make your first goal to have a friendly conversation with him or her.

Then when you reach your goal, make another goal. Lose five more pounds. Run two miles. Ask that special someone to go out for coffee.

Some goals are more useful when you set them high. If you're in school, make it your goal to get an A in every class. At work, make it your goal to be the top producer. If you reach your goal, then celebrate. If you miss, keep trying and be proud of your accomplishments. A missed goal is not a failure. It is simply an opportunity to set another goal and try again. Set your goal and let nothing stop you from achieving it.

"Three things in human life are important: the first is to be kind, the second is to be kind, and the third is to be kind."

— Henry James

SPIRITUAL · BE KIND

TAKE ACTION

Make it a point to perform at least one conscious act of kindness every day.

Kindness is the universal language. No matter where you go or with whom you interact, human beings respond to simple kindness. You don't need to speak the language or spend lots of money or flatter people. Your attitude of kindness will shine through.

I enjoy performing random acts of kindness. For example, whenever there is a serviceman or woman in line with me at the coffee shop, I always buy him or her a cup of coffee. I often do it for others as well. It never ceases to amaze me how this single small act can instantly transform a person's demeanor.

Kindness can be contagious. If you show kindness, it's much more likely that kindness will be shown to you. That grumpy woman at the store checkout? Give her a smile. The rude customer service person on the phone? Calm him with kindness. Your kindness could make a difference in their lives. They might even pass that kindness on to others.

Determine to develop an attitude of kindness. Go out of your way to be kind to everyone you meet. The kindness you show will be multiplied and returned to you in more ways than you can imagine.

Kindhearted
Indulgent
Neighborly
Devoted

"Constant complaint is the poorest sort of pay for all the comforts we enjoy."

— **Benjamin Franklin**

NEVER

TAKE ACTION

Stop whining!

What's bugging you? Your boss at work? A rude person at the coffee shop? The weather? To notice things that displease you is only human. It is natural to be aware of the world around you and its condition. Indeed, awareness can be a vital mechanism for self-preservation. In the jungle of life, you would not survive very long if you were not sensitive to your surroundings.

But to see defects and to verbalize your knowledge of them are two different things. To complain is to be inherently self-centered. The things that you see as faults are the same things that other people see and feel, too. There is no reason to point out the obvious. Instead of magnifying the negative, why not magnify the positive? Why not be a beacon of positive energy that gives hope and comfort to others?

If you train yourself to focus on the positive, you'll feel better about the world in general. Positivity reduces stress and, therefore, lowers blood pressure. When you are positive, you will be the person that people naturally gravitate toward, not the one they desperately avoid.

The statement "never complain" does not mean that we should avoid facing and overcoming life's challenges. We need to discuss the real issues with our family, friends, and co-workers. That's not complaining. That's life in all its glorious variety. Celebrate all of it. Complain about none of it.

"Let food be thy medicine, thy medicine shall be thy food."

— **Hippocrates**

PHYSICAL — **EAT RIGHT** — 46

EAT

TAKE ACTION

At your next meal, swap one unhealthy food item for something more wholesome.

We all need food and drink. And, being omnivores, our bodies are amazingly tolerant of what we consume. Meat, fish, grains, fruits, vegetables, oils—humans have eaten them all for thousands of years.

Today, most people in developed nations face a special challenge. According to the United States Department of Agriculture, the average adult needs between 1,800 and 2,200 calories per day to thrive. For most of us, eating this much food every day is no problem. Food is plentiful and cheap, and supermarkets are open day and night. We do not fear starvation. The problem we face is that we can easily consume twice this many calories, or more, every day. And that's not healthy.

To stay healthy, you have to eat right. How do you eat right? You prepare and eat healthy foods in moderation. It really is that simple. (Dining out is often one of the worst offenders in terms of healthy food and portion sizes.)

You don't need a lifelong diet plan to eat in a healthful manner. It can be as simple as making better decisions for your next meal. If you make the less refined, more natural, and whole foods choices, you can't go wrong. Some examples: Opt for a sweet potato instead of a white potato. Choose veggies instead of fries with your burger. Eat some strawberries instead of strawberry shortcake. Snack on yogurt instead of ice cream. Small changes in your diet will go a long way toward achieving the proper nutrition that your body needs.

"Forgiveness is the economy of the heart… forgiveness saves the expense of anger, the cost of hatred, the waste of spirits."

— Hannah More

FORGIVE

TAKE ACTION

If you need to forgive someone, do it now and free your mind and your soul.

Every once in a while we hear a news story about the victim of a horrible crime who has forgiven his perpetrator. We may think, how can he do that? Doesn't he want revenge—or at least payback of some sort?

When you think about it, forgiveness makes perfect sense. The past cannot be changed. Once an offense has been committed, it cannot be undone. A thoughtless comment, a lie, a deception, a theft—to varying degrees all of these are acts that hurt us or bring injury. Some are worse than others, and some bear lasting effects while others may fade. But all have happened, and none can be taken back.

Where does that leave the victim? It depends. When our hearts are consumed by the desire for payback, we are robbed of the joy of life. We cannot be free. The wrong committed against us may become a new driving force in our lives.

The act of unconditional forgiveness breaks those chains. It clears the air and the soul. We know that forgiving is not an endorsement of the wrongful act. Forgiving does not require us to socialize with the one who hurt us. We forgive to put the pain behind us so that we can heal. Then we can move forward in life with a clear head and happier heart.

"It is better to travel well than to arrive."

— **Buddha**

ROAD TRIP

50

PRACTICAL

TAKE ACTION

Check your calendar. When can you take a few days off? Mark the dates, get out a map and start planning your next road trip.

Ah, the joys of the open road. When life seems like an endless treadmill of work, eat, sleep, repeat, repeat, repeat, the best cure is to break the routine. Seek new horizons. Who knows what you will find over the next hill? It could be a historic site or a mesmerizing scenic view. Think of all the places there are to explore and new sights to see.

Some of the most memorable experiences happen "on the road". You probably have some special memories of road trips that you have taken. Even short ones are fun. Why not hike that new trail that you found on the map? How about a short drive to the new restaurant that recently opened a few towns away?

Don't be in a hurry to get to your destination. Many times, getting there is half the fun. These are ideal opportunities to catch up on conversations and reconnect with your spouse, children, or friends.

Don't have a car? Take a bike ride. Or hop on the train or a bus. However you choose to travel, a road trip can give you a fresh new perspective.

"What is tolerance? It is the consequence of humanity. We are all formed of frailty and error; let us pardon reciprocally each other's folly—that is the first law of nature."

— **Voltaire**

BE TOLERANT

SOCIAL

TAKE ACTION

Do some soul searching. Look for ways in which you are showing intolerance toward others and vow to make a change.

A study of history plainly reveals the terrible cost of intolerance. We can see it in how the Nazis treated the Jews (and anyone else they didn't like) in Germany during the World War II era. We can see it in our own country's unhappy history of race relations. We can see it in our high schools when kids who don't fit in are bullied. We may even see it at work or in our social lives when we don't give other people the respect they deserve based on something about them that we don't like.

Personal intolerance can manifest itself in very subtle ways. We exclude the guy because of his skin color. We don't promote someone who has a different religion. We stand aside when a bully lashes out at someone weaker. These small incidences of intolerance are like individual hailstones that fall in a storm. We may not notice one or two, but when they fall in a torrent, they inflict serious damage. Consider a young person who kills herself as a result of several small instances of bullying. Such stories are tragic examples of the destructive force of intolerance.

On the other hand, tolerance is empowering. When we accept other people for who they are, we open ourselves up to new experiences and understanding. Variety is the spice of life. Life would be dull indeed if everyone were the same. And think about what life would be like if the people around us did not accept us for who we are, warts and all.

"Music gives a soul to the universe, wings to the mind, flight to the imagination and life to everything."

— **Plato**

TAKE ACTION

Choose your instrument, find an instructor, and make some music.

Music is a powerful force. It can excite, soothe, enhance a romantic mood, or even help motivate a person to exercise. Anyone who has attended a concert has witnessed the way music can whip the crowd into a frenzy. And if you have ever listened to a lovely piece of music during a candlelit dinner or on a date, you know that it can transform an ordinary dining room into a magical place of romance.

We are voracious consumers of music. Many of us regard music as a commodity—something that is produced by other people and packaged and sold. Most of us are just consumers of this commodity called music. But what if music could become an even bigger part of our lives?

You can do more than just listen to music. You can make it. It's never too late to learn how to play a musical instrument. Guitar, piano, drums, flute, violin, banjo—the choices are vast. And the benefits of playing an instrument are many. Most simply, once you become proficient enough to play a simple tune, it becomes fun. You can play an instrument almost any time. Making music is a wonderful way to relax.

For children, the effects of learning how to play an instrument are profound. Musical training helps develop critical thinking skills and mental discipline. In order to play music, you need to grasp simple mathematical relationships, and kids do this without even realizing they are learning. Researchers at Northwestern University found that children who play music are better readers and have a larger vocabulary than children who don't play music.

Don't be just another music consumer; get involved and make your own music.

APPRECIATE OTHERS

SOCIAL

"Appreciation can make a day—even change a life. Your willingness to put it into words is all that is necessary."

— **Margaret Cousins**

APPRECIATE
thank you

TAKE ACTION

Make time to appreciate (and acknowledge) the selfless acts of others around you.

You may be unaware of all the things people do for you every day. If you're like most folks, you go about your day taking for granted the countless ways the acts of others make your life easier (and perhaps a bit sweeter).

How do others make my life easier, you ask? Consider the barista who knows exactly how you take your latte—and gets it for you super-fast when you're running late. Or how about the co-worker who covers for you so you can make your son's soccer game? Could you even have a career if your spouse didn't help you run errands, do the laundry, clean the house and prepare meals?

Every day, in countless ways, we benefit from being part of a larger society in which everyone plays a critical role. While we may consider some roles more important or perhaps more valuable than others, each of us has a vital contribution to make that deserves appreciation.

So what to do? Appreciate others. Tell your spouse how much you love him or her and how much you appreciate all he or she does for you. Buy your co-workers coffee and donuts to show them you value their contributions to your project. Send a note to a friend and emphasize his importance in your life. Show and express your appreciation to others who deserve (and need) it.

Others

"Never be too afraid, shy, embarrassed, proud or stubborn to ask for help."

— **Unknown**

TAKE ACTION

If you have a problem you can't solve, reach out and get help from a sympathetic friend or a qualified professional.

In the world's vast collection of legends and myths, we read of strong warriors who endure hardships, defeat the enemy, and ride off alone into the sunset. In our daily lives, we're encouraged to "tough it out" and to be self-reliant.

But there is a big difference between self-reliance and getting the help you need when you need it. If you broke your arm, would you set the break yourself? Of course not, you'd call a doctor. If your house caught on fire, would you try to put it out yourself? Certainly not, you'd call the fire department. If you wanted to learn how to fly an airplane, would you take off alone? No, you'd enroll in a flight school.

Personal challenges are no different. Many people suffer from depression or have substance abuse problems or find it difficult to cope with the stress of everyday life in general. These are the kinds of things you can't always solve by yourself. You may need the assistance of a person or group designed to help people just like you. Help may be just a phone call and an appointment away. Your job is to ask for it.

"What sunshine is to flowers, smiles are to humanity. These are but trifles, to be sure, but scattered along life's pathway, the good they do is inconceivable."

— **Joseph Addison**

SMILE OFTEN

60

SOCIAL

TAKE ACTION

Try this experiment. Go through your day with a big smile. Notice the effect it has on both you and others.

Smiling at the people around you may not seem important, but this simple act can make a big difference in your life and the lives of others. Consider this: everyone you meet is going through some issue, some crisis, or some stress. A smile from you gives that person a moment of respite. Your smile can remind a person that things are not that bad. It can show them that someone, even a stranger, cares enough to offer a bit of comfort. It's possible to alter another person's demeanor just by giving him or her a smile.

Smiling comes with selfish benefits as well. You almost certainly will get better restaurant service, friendlier business interchanges, and other benefits from nothing more than a smile. The surly waitress? Transform her attitude with kindness. The robotic bank teller? Give him a big smile to let him know that his condition is not contagious.

Scientific evidence points to a connection between how you conduct yourself on the outside and how you feel on the inside. According to a study by the British Dental Health Foundation, smiling can improve your mood. When you make an effort to smile, you establish a context for how you see the world and how the world sees you. Humans inherently would rather interact with a smiling individual than with someone who has a stoic or even unpleasant expression. Your genuine smile can (and will) brighten the world around you.

Often

"Giving up smoking is the easiest thing in the world. I know because I've done it thousands of times."

— Mark Twain

DON'T SMOKE

PHYSICAL

don't

TAKE ACTION

Kick the habit.

It's hard to believe that as recently as seventy-five years ago, cigarettes were marketed as healthful products. Doctors endorsed them, and smoking was an accepted part of everyday life. Many people of a certain age can remember when smoking was acceptable on airplanes and in doctors' waiting rooms.

Science has proven the danger of cigarettes and other tobacco products. In terms of your health, smoking is the most destructive habit you can have. It is the one habit that will guarantee you a short life filled with health issues including lung problems, cancer, heart disease, bronchitis, and emphysema. Smoking is not so cool when you are required to carry an oxygen tank everywhere you go, and you can't climb a single flight of stairs because your lungs are full of tar.

Nicotine, the primary brain-altering compound in cigarette smoke, is highly addictive. According to the National Institute on Drug Abuse, nicotine can be as addictive as other drugs of abuse (such as cocaine or heroin). When you see a poor guy slogging through a blizzard to get to the corner store to buy a pack of cigarettes, you know his addiction is as bad as any junkie.

If you've never smoked, don't start. If you do smoke, stop. Many products and services are available to help you quit. Try and try again until you succeed. Your family will thank you.

"The ideal of calm exists in a sitting cat."

— **Jules Renard**

TAKE ACTION

The next time you are faced with a challenge, decision or problem remember the first action step: stay calm.

One of the most astounding examples of calmness under pressure is the tale of Airline Captain Chesley "Sully" Sullenberger. On January 15th, 2009 US Airways Flight 1549 (departing from LaGuardia Airport) hit a flock of birds and was disabled. It was apparent that the plane would have to make a crash landing. Captain "Sully" did not panic. He remained cool and calm and took the steps necessary to guide the crippled craft to a safe ditching in the Hudson River. The plane sank, but every passenger survived. Imagine the outcome of this event had Captain "Sully" panicked and let his fear and emotions cripple him both mentally and physically. Everyone on the plane could have perished.

Most will never face such a clear-cut life-and-death situation; however, ordinary people often face situations that test them socially, emotionally, spiritually, and financially. And it's important to remain calm in these situations in order to make wise decisions. Those who become excited waste precious energy that could be used to get them through the current crisis. Panic clouds the ability to think clearly and reason logically, and thereby makes it almost impossible to choose the best course of action or make the best decision. You may never be called upon to ditch a plane in the river, but every day you face challenges large and small. How to overcome them? Stay calm.

"You know you've reached middle age when you want to see how long your car will last instead of how fast it will go."

— **Unknown**

CHANGE OIL 66 PRACTICAL

Change

TAKE ACTION

Check your oil or have it checked by a competent mechanic.

Cars used to be high-maintenance machines. As recently as ten or twenty years ago car owners had to do all sorts of things to keep their vehicles running smoothly: change the spark plugs, adjust the timing, lubricate the chassis. Sometimes reliability was an issue: radiators boiled over, tires went flat, batteries died. If you owned a car, you needed to have some basic knowledge of how the thing worked.

Cars today seem to require nothing more than an occasional trip to the gas station to fill up the tank. While today's cars last longer and can operate well for longer periods between maintenance, one important bit of upkeep cannot be denied—the oil change. Mechanics agree. The best thing that you can do to prolong the life of your car is change your oil according to the manufacturer's specifications (usually every three to five thousand miles).

Dirty oil causes excessive wear to the precision parts of your car's engine and will shorten its life. Changing your oil is a lot cheaper than repairing a worn-out engine. Most dealerships and garages offer a reasonable price for an oil change, so there's no excuse for not performing this most vital maintenance function.

Change the oil in your car regularly. Your car will thank you in the form of years of reliable service.

"A crust eaten in peace is better than a banquet partaken in anxiety."

— Aesop

control

TAKE ACTION

Start experimenting with stress-control methods to see what works for you. When you find an effective technique, make it a part of your daily life.

In our frenzied, fast-paced society, we face many challenges and reasons to worry. We feel as though our jobs are not secure. The international situation is precarious. Unhealthy messages inundate our children. Many of us lose sleep over retirement.

These pressures are challenging and even if we face them without flinching, they usually end up creating something needless that can be very damaging: stress.

In a dangerous situation, temporary stress can sharpen our senses and give us the jolt of adrenaline we need to fight or take flight. But chronic, prolonged stress is unhealthy. It may appear as nervousness, irritability, lack of sleep, overeating, high blood pressure, or even heart disease. Research presented recently by the American Psychological Association indicates that stress affects immune responses, which in turn affect how well the body heals itself. Regular stress can also increase a person's susceptibility to allergies, which occur when the body creates a strong immune response to something that's not dangerous, like pollen.

What to do? Try to see the whole picture and remember what's important in your life. In other words, don't sweat the small stuff. And take the time to de-stress. Enjoy a long walk on a nature path, sign up for a weekly yoga class, or kick up your feet and read a book. Eat right and get ample sleep. With a clear head and calm nerves, you'll be better able to overcome life's challenges.

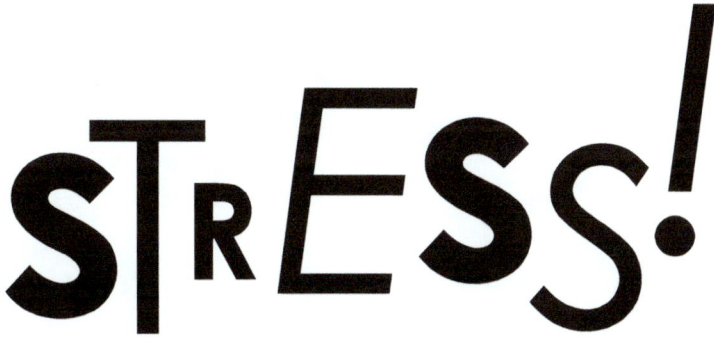

"You give but little when you give of your possessions. It is when you give of yourself that you truly give."

— **Kahlil Gibran**

TAKE ACTION

Develop a lifestyle of giving; pay it forward every chance you get.

Give everything? What? Are you suggesting we give everything away and live like beggars?

No, not exactly. What this means is that giving is important, and giving takes many forms. It means having a mind-set that is focused not on taking and consuming, but on contributing and giving back. The happiest people aren't those who write a check once a year to a charity and then congratulate themselves on their generosity while they dine on caviar at the country club. The way to achieve real joy is to make giving a part of your daily life.

One man who "gives everything" is a retired teacher named Allan Law. Allan is known as the "sandwich man" because he spends twelve hours a night delivering sandwiches to the homeless, poor and disadvantaged people of Minneapolis, Minnesota. He has been doing this every night since 1967.

We can't all be like Allan Law, but there are ways we can give everything. Offer to babysit your sister's children. Give up your seat on the bus to an expectant mom. Volunteer at a local soup kitchen. Coach little league baseball. Teach a Sunday school class. Organize a food drive.

Giving is something that we can do every day in many different ways. Each time we give, we feel that much better about ourselves. It's a win-win proposition.

Everything

"Walking is the best possible exercise. Habituate yourself to walk very far."

— **Thomas Jefferson**

WALK DAILY

TAKE ACTION

Go for a walk.

Human beings were made to move. Since the days of early humans, our ancestors roamed over fields and forests on their own two feet. They walked and ran and jumped and danced. Rare was the human who sat in one place all day.

Technological progress, while beneficial to modern man in countless ways, has brought with it a few drawbacks. One of these is an increasingly sedentary lifestyle. Unless you are one of the few who work on a farm or in a service occupation that requires you to be on your feet, you probably spend many hours a day sitting in your car, at your desk, or in a recliner at home.

The solution is simple. Get off the couch and move. Incorporate movement into your life every day. You don't have to engage in a full-blown workout program to garner the benefits of movement. If you normally take the elevator, climb the stairs. Park the car in the space farthest from your office door. Take a brisk fifteen-minute walk during your break at work.

According to the Mayo Clinic, daily movement will lower blood pressure, help you to control your weight, increase your levels of good cholesterol, reduce stress, and control your blood sugar. The benefits of even small increases in your daily movement are enormous. Take the first steps and begin walking your way toward a healthier lifestyle.

"Life is not about looking back and wishing that today is the same as the past. Life is about moving on, accepting changes and looking forward to what makes you stronger and more complete because it's never been too late to have a life and never too late to change one."

— **Unknown**

TAKE ACTION

Forget the past and all of its hurts, mistakes, and regrets. Look ahead to all that your future holds.

We all probably know someone who seems stuck in the past. Perhaps it's a relative, a neighbor, or a friend at work. This person may talk about the good old days and how everything was better yesteryear. Or she may take the opposite approach and complain about past ills—things that offended her such as an insult delivered by a thoughtless person.

Celebrating the past is healthy, and it's wise to learn lessons from experience. But the past, good or bad, is gone. You can't change it. If it was bad, you can't make it better. You certainly can't re-create or relive the special times. The past is nothing but history and memories. Keep the pleasant memories, and learn to live with or let go of the mistakes, regrets, and failures.

The future, however, is what you make it. Opportunities are waiting around the corner. New experiences await you in the future. There are goals to strive for, new skills to learn, worlds to explore. There are, as the saying goes, "places to go, people to meet, things to do." Your life lies in what's ahead—not what's behind. Go forward boldly to all your life that lies ahead.

"The strongest of all warriors are these two—Time and Patience."

— **Leo Tolstoy**

BE PATIENT

SPIRITUAL

Be

TAKE ACTION

Slow down, if only a little.

Many people in our modern world intend to get whatever they want in a hurry, whether it's a car, home, a significant other, or simply their way. We don't want to wait online or in traffic, and we certainly don't want to be put on hold on the telephone. We like that a mere mouse click on our computer can deliver a range of things from information, shopping, and conversation to entertainment—wherever and whenever we want.

But where is all of this convenience and speed getting us? One downside to instant gratification occurs when we get what we want too quickly and realize we've made a mistake. We did not think the situation through, and now we are stuck with the inappropriate vehicle, house, or significant other. Something else to consider: impatience breeds anxiety, frustration, and dissatisfaction.

Patience—on the other hand—creates confidence, decisiveness, and a rational outlook. Taking the time to think things through brings about peace of mind. In some cases, the only way to ensure success is to learn patience. Farmers know that you have to wait until just the right moment to harvest the crops. Children need much time and attention to mature into productive young adults. New companies require time to become profitable.

So ask yourself, why am I in such a hurry? Then take the long way to work on purpose. Make a home-cooked meal instead of going for fast food. Welcome the relaxation that comes with taking your time.

PATIENT

"A penny here and a dollar there, placed at interest, goes on accumulating, and in this way the desired result is attained. It requires some training, perhaps, to accomplish this economy, but when once used to it, you will find there is more satisfaction in rational saving than in irrational spending."

— P. T. Barnum

TAKE ACTION

Next payday, before doing anything else, take a portion of your check and place it in your savings account. Repeat every payday.

The first decade of this new century marks a period when many Americans borrowed too much, bought too much stuff on credit, and became financially overextended. We wound up with massive credit card and consumer debt when the economy tanked. We thought the good times would keep on rolling, and we would have no problem paying our bills.

The hard lessons of the recession have changed our thinking. We now recognize the concept of saving. We once again make purchases using layaway plans, a concept that had fallen by the wayside for decades.

But we still have a long way to go. According to the Federal Bureau of Economic Analysis, American families saved a respectable 11.1 percent of their family income in 1985. By 2006, that figure plummeted to negative 0.4 percent. In 2009, it crept back up to 1.2 percent. Better, but not good enough. In France, families save a whopping 12.3 percent of their income. In Germany—a country that has escaped the worst of the recession—families have consistently saved more than 10 percent.

Target to save a minimum of 10 percent of your take-home pay. If you can't start at 10 percent, find a lower percentage you feel comfortable with and try to increase it at regular intervals until you reach or surpass that 10 percent figure.

Saving is important—for retirement, for college, or for a special vacation. Put a little away every week, and you'll build financial security for yourself and your family.

"Sunburn is nature's way of telling us not to go outside."

— **Unknown**

PHYSICAL | **SUN BLOCK** | 80

TAKE ACTION

Embrace the outdoors, but remember to block the sun.

The sun is the source of all the energy on earth. It provides our planet with light and heat. It is a source of life for plants and animals alike. Without the sun's light, many humans become depressed. The sun is also essential for vitamin D production.

However, too much sun can be a problem. Overexposure to the sun's rays can damage our skin, prematurely age the skin, and increase the risk of skin cancer. Too much sun can also damage our eyes. The solution is not to remain indoors; we humans need sunshine. The solution is to block the sun. Apply sunscreen on your skin and shield your eyes from the sun's strong rays.

To protect your eyes, buy the best pair of sunglasses that you can afford. You need sunglasses that offer 100 percent UV protection. Polarization (which significantly reduces glare from flat surfaces such as a road or body of water) is a personal choice, but many people find they see more clearly with polarized sunglasses.

As for sunscreen, hundreds of products are available, and you can pay as much or as little as you want. Independent testing by Consumer Reports has shown little correlation between the price of a particular sunscreen and the protection it offers. The generic brands can be just as effective as the name brands. You need a sunscreen that offers both UVA and UVB protection. Wear sunscreen year-round, not just in the summer. Apply it liberally and reapply after sweating or swimming. Contrary to all the advertising, there is no such thing as a waterproof sunscreen.

"There is not a passion so strongly rooted in the human heart as envy."

— **Richard Brinsley Sheridan**

SPIRITUAL | **DON'T ENVY**

don't

TAKE ACTION

Transform your envy into ambition and action.

Both experts and philosophers agree: envy is a complex emotion. Words used to describe it include unreasonable, irrational, and vicious. Envy has been known to inspire people to lie, cheat, steal—and take even more dreadful actions.

No one wants to envy another, and yet it happens. Someone you know buys the car you desire. A woman at work clinches the position you've worked toward for years. A guy you know from college has the perfect life you once imagined for yourself.

Some psychologists suggest that there may be two types of envy: malicious envy, which is destructive and promotes low self-esteem; and benign envy, which can be a positive motivational force.

Malicious envy is the misery that comes when you perceive someone has something that you don't have, but wish you did. This emotion may fire off other negative emotions like jealousy, distrust, and hatred. It is this envy that you ultimately want to remove from your life. It is destructive to both your emotional and physical health.

But if you stop and recognize that you are focusing on the things you don't have, you can turn envy into something positive. You can change the malicious envy to benign envy. In other words, use your envy to inspire your ambition.

Consider that it's possible for you to get that car, job, or life, if you take the steps to work toward it. Simply chart a course that leads to achieving the thing you want most. Know that you can do it if you try.

"If you want to lift yourself up, lift up someone else."

— **Booker T. Washington**

build

TAKE ACTION

Use the leverage of your words and actions to build up others.

Most everyone knows a friend or colleague who lives to point out the flaws in other people's accomplishments. You know the one: The co-worker who is the first to spot an error on your presentation. The parent who complains that his child scored just one goal and not two at soccer. The friend who always manages to let you know he makes more money than you.

Perhaps you are this person. Don't be. It's an existence filled with negativity, an attitude that ensures you will never be content. There is no joy in this outlook, no personal satisfaction at all.

Wouldn't you rather be the person that people gravitate to for motivation and support—the one who builds people up rather than tearing them down? Certainly you would. It's infinitely better to help people reach a goal than it is to point out the reasons they aren't reaching it. Everyone wins when they focus on their strengths and when they believe their efforts will see positive results.

In the workplace, reward superior performance. At home, help family members set goals for themselves and applaud when they reach those goals. In the community, promote worthy causes. Build people up every chance you get and watch what happens in their lives, and yours.

"Camp out among the grass and gentians of glacier meadows, in craggy garden nooks full of Nature's darlings. Climb the mountains and get their good tidings. Nature's peace will flow into you as the sunshine flows into the trees. The winds will blow their freshness into you, and the storms their energy, while cares will drop off like autumn leaves."

— **John Muir**

Get

TAKE ACTION

Go for a short walk outside. Enjoy the sights, sounds, and smells of nature.

Human beings have not always spent so much time enclosed within four walls. When you consider the grand scheme of things, it has only been a few thousand years that we've built homes and offices to live and work inside. Before that, we were outdoors people, dwelling in forests and sleeping in caves—at one with the earth.

So it makes sense that getting outdoors can naturally make a person feel better—especially if you're having one of those claustrophobic, hectic, "can't wait to get out of work" days. The sunlight alone tickles the receptors in your brain and inspires a pleasant mood. Pair that with a crisp breeze through the trees and the feel of dirt or grass below the feet, and you might momentarily forget your gripping anxieties.

Getting outdoors is an ideal way to remind yourself that something bigger is out there: bigger than you, bigger than your job, bigger than whatever problems ail you. The mere sight of the open sky carrying on for miles upon miles should be enough to remind you of your place (and your troubles' places) in this universe.

If you've been looking at the same four walls for too long, change your focus. Get outdoors. Go for a long hike. Better yet, go camping. Trek into a remote campsite and when darkness falls, lie back and count the stars. Listen to the night sing. Breathe the clean air. Enjoy all the peace and tranquility that the outdoors can offer.

"My life has been full of terrible misfortunes most of which never happened."

— **Michel de Montaigne**

don't

TAKE ACTION

What are you worried about? Ask yourself this question, "Is there anything I can do to resolve the issue or help the situation?" If the answer is no, then stop worrying.

It's a simple expression popularized by a smiley face and a pop song. For many folks, it's easy to dismiss "don't worry" as a simplistic balm suitable perhaps only for children.

But if you dig a little deeper, you will find a gem. In the Bible, the book of Matthew chapter, 6, verses 25 and 34 address the subject: "Therefore I tell you, do not worry about your life, what you will eat or drink; or about your body, what you will wear. Is not life more than food, and the body more than clothes? Can any one of you by worrying add a single hour to your life?"

The underlying message is that worrying is a profoundly unproductive activity. No one ever solved a problem, raised a child, or built a business by worrying. To fret over problems that might occur in the future will not change that future or help you face those problems. When the weather bureau announces that a hurricane is coming, will worrying make you safe? No. In fact, it will make you less safe because you will have wasted your energy when you should have got to work making preparations.

Don't worry. Do the very best you can every day, and when a challenge comes, you'll be ready.

"Water is the only drink for a wise man."

— **Henry David Thoreau**

DRINK WATER

90

PHYSICAL

TAKE ACTION

Get up now and grab a glass of water. Your body will use it wisely.

The shelves of supermarkets and convenience stores are bulging with a variety of beverages: soft drinks, sports drinks, energy drinks, juices. Every street corner boasts a specialty coffee shop where we can get a fancy sugar-laden concoction for five dollars. Vending machines stand ready to dispense cans of caffeinated power drinks and calorie-filled sodas.

Amidst this bounty of processed beverages, it's easy to forget that our bodies crave the refreshment (and nourishment) of water. In fact, water is the largest single component of our bodies. The total amount of water in a person who weighs 150 pounds is approximately 10.5 gallons, representing an average of 57 percent of total body weight. In babies, water may be as high as 75 percent of total body weight. Obesity reduces the percentage of water in the body, sometimes to as low as 45 percent.

Water is vital to the functioning of all of your critical internal organs, especially the brain. With the loss of only 2 percent of your body's water, dehydration (characterized by headache, tiredness, dizziness, and irritability) can set in. Dehydration can cause an increasing sense of confusion, fatigue, and negative moods. The proper amount of hydration is critical to your overall health, and there is no better beverage for hydration than water.

Water

"With malice toward none, with charity for all, with firmness in the right as God gives us to see the right, let us strive on to finish the work we are in, to bind up the nation's wounds, to care for him who shall have borne the battle and for his widow and his orphan, to do all which may achieve and cherish a just and lasting peace among ourselves and with all nations."

— **Abraham Lincoln**

Make

TAKE ACTION

Determine in your heart, mind, and soul that you will be a peacemaker.

The phrase "make peace" contains an active verb: make. It's a word we know very well. As a society and as individuals, we make things all the time: cars, houses, cell phones, TV shows, works of art, fashions. All of these things comprise the products of our culture.

Sadly, we often make war, too. Like anything else we make, this requires resources and effort. If the war is significant enough, it can require the combined efforts of an entire nation.

Peace, of course, is our preference, and we all recognize it as such. But we often do not recognize that peace is not just the absence of conflict. It is not always passive. We have to make peace the same way we make anything else. Peace requires resources and hard work. It often requires courage, personal sacrifice, and purposeful action.

Making peace can be done both on a national level and a personal one. Each one of us can make peace—with our family, with our neighbors, and even with ourselves. In fact, making peace with ourselves is probably the most important thing we can do. If you don't make peace with yourself, it will be difficult to make peace with anyone else. With whom you need to "make peace"? Yourself? Others? Do it now and experience a newfound contentment in your life.

"Blessed is he who expects nothing, for he shall never be disappointed."

— **Alexander Pope**

EXPECT NOTHING

MENTAL

expect

TAKE ACTION

Find something you love to do. Make it your passion. Expect nothing but the satisfaction of a job well done.

It is a central tenet of Buddhism that desire is the root of suffering. By desire, Buddhists mean the state of craving pleasure, material goods, and immortality, all of which are wants that can never be satisfied. As a result, desiring them can only bring suffering.

However, it cannot be denied that human beings have an innate desire to accomplish, achieve, and accumulate. We strive to attain new goals. These goals may be material (a new car), spiritual (to be happier), or communal (to cure disease). We are satisfied when we reach our goals and unsatisfied when we do not. It is this sense of dissatisfaction that drives us forward to new accomplishments and new heights.

How can we believe that desire is the root of suffering, and yet recognize that desire drives us forward? By embracing not the product but the process. Have you ever wondered why folks like Warren Buffet and Bill Gates don't retire? Clearly, financial security is not an issue. They understand that the process of creating wealth (for themselves and others) is more important, more rewarding, than the actual wealth itself.

We humans like to keep busy. We invent things, fix things, engage in business, play sports, and create art. We help our neighbors. And at the end of the day, we know that our labors will never end. There will always be more to do, and we may not receive a reward for our efforts. That's OK. If we pursue our goals purely for personal satisfaction, then we will never be disappointed.

"When you arise in the morning, think of what a precious privilege it is to be alive—to breathe, to think, to enjoy, to love."

— **Marcus Aurelius**

TAKE ACTION

Make a determined effort to be positive today. Watch the effect it has on you and the world around you.

"When You're Smiling" is a song made famous by the legendary musician Louis Armstrong. The advice he gave in this song must have worked for him. Despite a very rough childhood and the hardships of racial discrimination, Armstrong achieved a career and success that few others have.

But Armstrong wasn't telling folks simply to paste a big grin on their faces. His message was to be positive and to radiate what a later generation called "good vibrations". Positive people do not dwell on their misfortunes. They do not see themselves as powerless in the hands of fate. They face each new day with optimism and strength, and help others overcome life's obstacles.

Being positive has health benefits. As the Mayo Clinic reports, your attitude toward yourself, and whether you're optimistic or pessimistic, may affect your health. Health benefits related to optimism include lower incidents of depression, reduced risk of death from heart problems, and improved immunity. All of these benefits can lead to a longer lifespan.

Positive thinking doesn't mean that you ignore life's challenges, keep your head in the sand, and see only the good things. Positive thinking means that you handle bad news in a more positive and productive way, that you don't dwell on the negatives, and that you hope for the best. When you think the best is going to happen, you increase the odds that it will. Change your thinking and you'll change the outcome. Be positive.

POSI+IVE

"Conservation means development as much as it does protection. I recognize the right and duty of this generation to develop and use the natural resources of our land; but I do not recognize the right to waste them, or to rob, by wasteful use, the generations that come after us."

— **Theodore Roosevelt**

TAKE ACTION

Find a way to incorporate recycling into your daily life. The future of our existence on this planet depends on it.

We hear the word *sustainability* all the time. Have you ever stopped to think of what it means to you, your children, your grandchildren? Sustainability means using the earth's resources in ways that will allow for the viability of future generations. Experts predict that we will need to significantly reduce our dependence on the earth's natural resources if we are to continue life on this planet as we now know it. The answer—reduce, reuse, and recycle.

Most of us consume a lot of stuff. Food products, clothing, paper, bottles, packaging. All of it comes into our homes, and the majority of it leaves via the trash can. According to the Annenberg Foundation, the average American generates four pounds of solid trash per day, for a total of 1,460 pounds per year. Every day, Americans throw away approximately two hundred million tons of trash. Less than one-quarter of it is recycled, leaving the rest to landfills and incinerators.

In the past decade, we've made significant progress, especially with staple items such as paper. Nearly 40 percent of the fiber used to make new paper products in the United States comes from recycled sources. In 2012, the paper industry's goal was to recover (for recycling) 60 percent of all the paper Americans consume. That is approximately sixty million tons of paper.

There is still much to do. Every family can make a difference by reducing the amount of trash they toss out. Many communities offer recycling services along with the regular trash pickup. You can sort glass bottles, metal cans, most plastics, cardboard, and paper products for recycling. You can also compost food and even recycle rainwater to use in your garden. Make a commitment to do your part and recycle everything you can.

EVERYTHING

"You are not here merely to make a living. You are here to enable the world to live more amply, with greater vision, a finer spirit of hope and achievement. You are here to enrich the world, and you impoverish yourself if you forget the errand."

— **Woodrow Wilson**

GIVE

TAKE ACTION

Make a list of ways in which you and your family can give back. Take action on one of them this week.

It's nice to receive gifts on your birthday or a holiday. It feels good to know that friends and family are thinking of you.

Imagine, then, how your gifts make other people feel. It's rewarding to give someone a special gift and to experience his or her reaction to receiving it.

There are many ways you can give back in life. Of course, there is the obvious way, which is to give a gift publicly. Perhaps you have made a donation to a favorite charity and have received recognition. That's wonderful. But sometimes the most rewarding way to give is quietly and anonymously. The most meaningful gifts are often those given without the expectation of acknowledgment.

Donations and gifts are one way to give back, but how about volunteering your time and talent? Volunteering is an admirable way to share your gifts with others.

You are an awesome combination of skills, talent, personality, and expertise. Your unique abilities and capabilities were not meant just to enhance your position in life. You were designed to invest your life to enrich the lives of others. Find a way to do this, and you will enrich your life too.

BACK

> "Shabelsky: Doctors are the same as lawyers, the sole difference being that lawyers only rob you, but doctors rob you and kill you too."
>
> — **Anton Chekhov,** *Ivanov*

GET CHECKUPS

PHYSICAL

102

GET

TAKE ACTION

Even if you feel fine, be sure to have your doctor check under the hood every year.

Did you ever have a friend or neighbor who bought a car and never did any maintenance on it? Never checked the oil or changed the air filter? Never put air in the tires? "That stuff isn't important," he would say. "When my car breaks down I'll get it fixed."

Sure enough, one day his car broke down. Not some little thing, but something big. The car needed major, costly repairs. "I never saw it coming," your friend said as he maxed out his credit card at the auto repair shop. If your friend had taken his car to the shop for regular maintenance, chances are the mechanic would have spotted the problem before it grew to such large proportions.

Your body is no different. It, too, can develop problems that don't immediately show. Diseases such as cancer, clogged arteries, and hypertension can be present without symptoms. However, if you get an annual physical from your family physician, you may catch a disease in its early stages. A regular checkup can prevent minor problems from becoming major issues. A regular checkup is vital to your overall health and well-being.

Checkups

"Do not forsake wisdom, and she will protect you; love her, and she will watch over you. Wisdom is supreme; therefore get wisdom. Though it cost all you have, get understanding."

— **Holy Bible: New International Version**

TAKE ACTION

Make it a point to study and emulate the qualities that you find in those who have extraordinary wisdom.

Wisdom is not for wizards and sages alone. The desire to know and understand is a universal calling, and many people answer that call by striving for a broad foundation of knowledge.

Wisdom is more than intelligence. It is the integration of knowledge, experience, and deep understanding. Those who seek wisdom in their lives can achieve a sense of calm. Their more peaceful attitude comes from the belief that viable solutions exist for even life's toughest problems. In other words, the more you know about the world, the more potential solutions you see for solving the world's troubles. On a personal level, instead of worrying about his problems, a wise person asks himself, "How can I solve my problems?"

Wisdom brings with it a tolerance for life's natural ups and downs. When you truly believe everything can and will work out in the end, you have no need to panic. Times may be tough, but because you have studied the history of the world, you remain confident that things will get better.

How can you gain wisdom? Perhaps one way is to find a few people that you think have considerable wisdom and study them thoroughly. Are they easily excited? Do they make spontaneous decisions or do they deliberate and seek counsel? Are they judgmental or tolerant? Do they listen more than they talk? Make these folks your role models, and you've taken the first steps toward becoming wise.

> "Nothing in the world can take the place of persistence. Talent will not; nothing is more common than unsuccessful men with talent. Genius will not; unrewarded genius is almost a proverb. Education alone will not; the world is full of educated derelicts. Persistence and determination alone are omnipotent."
>
> — Calvin Coolidge

Persevere

Continue in a course of action even in the face of **DIFFICULTY** or with little or no indication of success

PERSEVERE ALWAYS

MENTAL

TAKE ACTION

Never, never, never quit.

Most of us know of Vincent van Gogh as one of the greatest artist of all time. However, did you know that throughout his life, he struggled to sell his artwork? He suffered through bouts of serious physical and mental illness. His romantic relationships were a mess. Despite his trials and troubles, he continued to paint, draw and sketch, producing over 2,100 pieces of art. Although never viewed as a master artist during his lifetime, his work had a tremendous influence on later artists. In May of 1990, one of van Gogh's works sold for $82.5 million.

How often do we see this sort of persistence in our daily lives? The smooth-talking hotshot at work burns out while the hard worker rises to the top and becomes the CEO. The kid who is on the second-string football team in college keeps working on his game and makes the pros. The parents who give their kids daily attention and support see their offspring grow to become happy and productive adults. The student who puts forth her best effort day after day becomes class valedictorian.

Ask any successful person what the most important ingredient to success is, and you will probably get the same answer: perseverance. You must have perseverance because success is simply a string of failures pieced together. Thomas Edison once said, "Our greatest weakness lies in giving up. The most certain way to succeed is to try just one more time."

If a goal is worth reaching, it's worth a determined and focused effort. Set your goal, chart your course, and let nothing stand in your way.

ALWAYS

"A journey of a thousand miles begins with a single step."

— Lao Tzu

TAKE ACTION

What do you want to accomplish? Take one baby step toward your goal every day this week.

When Christopher Columbus sailed west across the ocean toward unknown lands, he embarked on a grand journey. In his case, a giant leap paid off, and he reached land. It's wise to remember that Columbus had no choice—his project could be undertaken only in one big step. For most of us, progress comes by setting small goals that we are confident we can attain.

When faced with a big project, it may seem intimidating until we break it into smaller pieces. Let's say you want to lose ten pounds. That seems like a lot. It's much more realistic to set a goal of losing one pound. Then, when you reach that goal, set another goal—one more pound. Reach that attainable goal ten times, and you've arrived.

Baby steps—it's how small businesses grow, often starting in a basement or garage. Perhaps the first baby step is to sell your product at the corner market near your home. It's a goal you can easily achieve. The next goal is to sell online. Easy enough. Your next goal is to sell your product in twenty stores in your region. And so it goes, until your series of baby steps covers a distance you never thought imaginable.

The only way to make permanent changes in your life is to make small changes and develop them into permanent habits. Whether you want to start exercising, play an instrument, or earn a degree, the process is the same. Begin with a small change, cultivate it into a habit, and build on that habit with the next small change.

You can get anywhere you want to be if you take enough baby steps.

THANKS

Ask any author what it takes to write a book and he or she will probably tell you that a book is a collaboration of the efforts of many. It may be the author's unique original idea, but it truly takes a team effort to bring a final product to fruition.

A special thank you goes out to Thomas Hauck, Kim Catanzarite, David Locke, and all the incredibly talented folks at Locke Design.

A final thank you goes out to all those who have had a part, however big or small, in the creation of this work. It's been an amazing experience.

www.ingramcontent.com/pod-product-compliance
Lightning Source LLC
Chambersburg PA
CBHW040554010526
44110CB00054B/2684